Ignite a Firestorm!

Using Dance to Reach Youth in Your Community

Ignite a Firestorm! Using Dance to Reach Youth in Your Community

Copyright © 2007 by Kelli J. Moore

Published by OneSource Productions
All requests for information should be addressed to 906 St. Lucie West Blvd., # 105, St. Lucie West, Fl 34986
ISBN # 978-0-6151-4827-4
Printed in the United States of America by Lulu.com

Unless otherwise noted, Scripture taken from the HOLY BIBLE, NEW INTERNATIONAL VERSION®. Copyright © 1973, 1978, 1984 International Bible Society. Used by permission of Zondervan. All rights reserved.

The "NIV" and "New International Version" trademarks are registered in the United States Patent and Trademark Office by International Bible Society. Use of either trademark requires the permission of International Bible Society.

Scripture quotations marked (AMP) are taken from the *Amplified Bible*, Copyright © 1954, 1958, 1962, 1964, 1965, 1987 by The Lockman Foundation. Used by permission.

Wired: For a Life of Worship by Louis Giglio. Published by Multnomah Books. Copyright © 2006 by Louis Giglio. All Rights Reserved.

Personality Plus: How to Understand Others by Understanding Yourself by Florence Littauer. Published by Fleming H. Revell, Copyright © 1992 by Florence Littauer. All Rights Reserved.

The Five Love Languages by Gary Chapman, Published by Northfield Publishers, Copyright © 1995 by Gary Chapman. All Rights Reserved.

The Heart of the Artist by Rory Noland. Published by Zondervan. Copyright © 1999 by Rory Noland. All Rights Reserved.

Who Moved My Cheese by Spencer Johnson, M.D. Published by G.P. Putnam's Sons. Copyright © 1998 by Spencer Johnson, M.D. All Rights Reserved.

Secret Keeper 2005: The Delicate Power of Modesty by Dannah Gresh. Published by Moody Publishing. Copyright © 2005 by Dannah Gresh. All Rights Reserved.

MySpace.com content is protected by copyright, trademark, patent, trade secret and other laws, and MySpace.com owns and retains all rights in the MySpace.com Content and the MySpace Services.

YouTube.com content is protected by copyright, trademark, patent, trade secret and other laws, and YouTube.com owns and retains all rights in the YouTube.com Content and the YouTube Services

---

Professional Photography provided by Nancy Cumba-Johnson of *Treasure Coast Talent Management.* TCTM1@yahoo.com

FireDance is a program of New Life Christian Centre and Firehouse Youth Centre, located in Port St. Lucie, FL.   www.nlcctoday.com   www.myfhyc.com

Acknowledgements

Most importantly, I thank God for his amazing grace and guidance in my life. It is because of Him and Him alone that our dance ministry has touched so many lives and this book was possible. May His Glory always shine through me and this ministry.

Special thanks also go to the countless people that have been involved in our ministry: Pastors Ron & Linda McCaskill and the staff of New Life Christian Centre (especially James & Deidre Turner, David Adair, John Paquette & Traci Helton) for your constant support and the opportunities you provide for the kids to dance; Danielle Bouloy, Jill Carillo & Lisa Kohler for your passion for dance and your faithfulness to this ministry; Nic & Misty Khoury for igniting the firestorm that is now known as FireDance; Moki Stewart for being a willing vessel and trailblazer in using hip hop dance for God; all the kids' parents who so faithfully support your children and this ministry (there are too many to name individually); the Ministry Team, each of whom have been willing to commit several hours each week to furthering their gifts and using them for God's glory; and their parents, who without hesitation provide transportation, uniforms, finances, time and most importantly, intercessory prayer for this ministry. Thanks also go out to those who provided feedback on this book and helped in the editing process: Eileen Brydebell, Nancy Johnson, Moki Stewart, Danielle Bouloy and Jennifer Krueger. Your insight was very helpful and I appreciate you more than you know.

My family has been an incredible source of encouragement for me as I've written this book and I thank God for them daily: my loving husband, Allen; my children, to whom God has given the gift of dance, Devin, Parker & Morgan; my parents, Ed & Judy Douglas and my brother, Kyan Douglas. God has blessed me very much with all of you – I love you.

This book is dedicated to the kids in our dance program and other Christian dance programs that, by faith, will be ignited throughout our world. May the name of Jesus be exalted in all that you do to reach youth in your communities.

Ignite a Firestorm!

Using Dance to Reach Youth in Your Community

By: Kelli J. Moore

"Praise Him with tambourine and [single or group] dance; praise Him with stringed and wind instruments or flutes!"
Psalm 150:4 (Amp)

Introduction

God placed a burden in our Pastor's heart over 8 years ago to start a contemporary dance program within our children and youth ministries. We had a few false starts over a 2 year period before committed lay people took up the task and pulled our first FireDance team together. We had eight kids, ages 7-10, none of whom had ever stepped into a dance class before.

Six years later, we have a variety of hip hop, breakdance and expressive teams as well as a Ministry Team (our version of a company team). The original directors have moved on to follow God's calling in another place, but because of the way the program was structured, the vision continues to be a reality.

Each step along the path was new territory for us and we were almost never qualified to do what was being asked. However, God's grace is more than sufficient and He always provided the resources we needed to go above and beyond expectations.

As we have continued to expand our dance program to reach more youth in our area, God has expanded our dream tremendously. We have a vision that includes seeing dance programs being used around the world to reach today's youth for Jesus.

I'm sure that God has also given you a vision for your ministry or you wouldn't be reading this right now. Wherever you are in your journey to establish a God-centered dance program, I believe that this book will help you along the way.

May God bless and keep you,

Kelli

Contents

Why Dance?
    Does Dance Belong in the Church?   Pg 2
    Is Dance Considered Worship?   Pg 4

Making It Work for You
    What Does Leadership Think?   Pg 8
    Reasons to Add Dance to the Program   Pg 9
    Reaching Today's Youth   Pg 10

How to Start
    How to Start   Pg 14
    On Your Mark   Pg 15
    Get Set   Pg 16
    GO!   Pg 16

Ten Keys to a Successful Program
    Key #1: Keep God the Focus   Pg 20
    Key #2: Enthusiasm!   Pg 21
    Key #3: TEAMwork   Pg 22
    Key #4: Create a Sense of Ownership   Pg 23
    Key #5: Raise up Leaders Within   Pg 23
    Key #6: Strive for Excellence   Pg 26
    Key #7: Be Flexible!   Pg 27
    Key #8: Never Compromise Your Values   Pg 28
    Key #9: Communicate Well   Pg 29
    Key #10: Have Fun!   Pg 31

Opportunities for Ministry
    Opportunities Are Everywhere   Pg 34
    A Final Word of Encouragement with Pictures!   Pg 37

Resources
    Team-building Games   Pg 44
    Devotion Ideas   Pg 47
    Music Ideas   Pg 49
    Dance Conferences   Pg 51
    Instructional Videos   Pg 53

Why Dance?

Chapter 1

Does Dance Belong in the Church?

If you are thinking of starting a contemporary dance ministry, then I'm assuming that you believe that dance is an acceptable way to worship. Hopefully you understand two things: 1) that God created all things and 2) all of the things that He created were created for His pleasure. There are some that would not agree that dance (and especially more contemporary styles like hip hop) has been created for God's pleasure, but to that I would counter that the Bible says that ALL things were created by and for God (Colossians 1:16) – so why not dance? There are several references in the Bible to dance being used as an act of worship, praise and celebration. Psalms 149 and 150 demonstrate acts of praise including singing, tambourines and dance. Even throughout the New Testament various references to rejoicing in the Lord refer back to dancing, when the original text is translated.

As the Creator of everything, God intended music and dance to be used for His glory. Unfortunately, the world has distorted and perverted some styles of dance into something tasteless and far from a worshipful experience. God is calling us to bring the true worship experience of dance to this generation of young people.

Let me state here that I am not addressing this issue from a specific denomination's perspective. Each church has its own guidelines regarding what's acceptable in adult and youth worship services. I'm looking at this issue from a Biblical perspective; as non-denominational as I can. I must also warn you that you may uncover some resistance to your ministry. Please understand that it's not personal; however, it's peoples' own limited thinking and lack of knowledge that causes them to fear. Using contemporary dance styles like hip hop in church may be a radical thought to some; especially those who feel that hip hop is inherently sinful. While I'll agree that several of the originators of the musical style we now call hip hop were islanders that believed in a voodoo religion, I'll point you back to my original statement in this chapter—God created ALL things and for God ALL things were created. Just because Satan has used this genre of music to further his campaign doesn't mean that as Christians we can't take it back into our camp and use it for God's glory!!

Many have asked if it's appropriate to use our current culture's musical style in Christian music. The same question was asked when the hard-rock style of music was used in Christian songs a few years ago. However, now it is widely accepted and used in many classic praise and worship songs. Looking back through history you'll see that the contemporary music of the time was often used to create the hymns that we now cherish as "good Christian music." As a matter of fact, Martin Luther used the current musical tunes of his time as the basis for many of his hymns. And don't forget the good ol' black gospel hymns that found their musical origins in "juke joints" all throughout the South. Even the music for *"Amazing Grace"* has been attributed to an old folk song, the contemporary music of that time.

Several of today's Christian artists have successfully created a phenomenal pop and/or hip hop sound while making sure that the message is pulled directly from the pages of God's Word. What's really exciting is how God is using this style of music and dance to reach youth all over this world. This book isn't about establishing a "hip hop church," where every aspect of the service is following this theme. It's about taking Christian lyrics with a good beat and putting choreography to them for the purpose of praising God in a way that is relevant to today's youth. There are currently active dance programs in many different church denominations. They simply incorporate this style of ministry into outreach efforts and their regular services.

Congratulations on taking this first step in exploring a way to incorporate today's culture into your worship experience. It's a great outreach tool and also brings tremendous energy to your adult and youth services.

Is Dance Considered Worship?

Like most of you, I knew that the word "dance" was mentioned in the Bible. Who hasn't heard the account of David dancing before the Lord upon the return of the Ark of the Covenant as described in 2 Samuel 6:14? Psalms 149:3 and 150:4 are two other familiar verses that describe dance in the Bible. However, as I began researching for this book, I found several other words written in the original Hebrew and Greek that when translated, indicate some form of movement that is used in dance. Every one of these words can be found in the Strong's Concordance, with definitions and Scripture references.

Here are a few Hebrew words that were used in the original writings of the Old Testament to express dancing, rejoicing, praising and worshipping of God, and the scripture verse(s) in which they can be found.

- **Chiyl** - twist or whirl (Judges 21:21)
- **Machowl** – a dance. (Psalm 30:11, Jeremiah 31:4)
- **Mechowlah** – a company of dancers. (Judges 11:34, Exodus 15:20)
- **Dalag, Raqad & Pazaz** – leap (Song of Solomon 2:8, Isaiah 35:6, 1 Chronicles 15:29, Ecclesiastes 3:4, 2 Samuel 6:16)
- **Pacach** – hop, skip over, to dance (1 Kings 18:26)
- **Giyl / Guwl** – spin around under the influence of emotion, usually rejoicing. (1 Chronicles 16:31, Psalm 9:14)
- **Alats** – jump for joy (Proverbs 28:12, Psalm 68:3)
- **Hallah** – praise and celebration. (1 Chronicles 16:4, Ezra 3:11)

Now consider these Greek words that were used in the New Testament to express dancing, rejoicing, praising and worshipping of God.

- **Orcheo** – leap with regularity of motion. (Matthew 11:17)
- **Choros** – a round dance (Luke 15:25)

- ❖ **Agalliao** – jump for joy, rejoice (Matthew 5:12, Revelation 19:7)
- ❖ **Skirtao** – jump for joy (Luke 1:41, Luke 6:23)
- ❖ **Proskuneo** – worship, prostrate oneself in homage (John 4:23, Revelation 7:11)
- ❖ **Latreuo** – to service, minister, worship (Philippians 3:3, Luke 2:37)

Paul tells us in the book of 1 Corinthians that Christians are a temple of the Holy Spirit and that we should glorify God with our bodies. He also tells us in Romans 12 that we should offer our bodies as a living sacrifice, holy and pleasing to God because it is our spiritual act of worship. As you can see, God Himself gives us several reasons in His Word to believe that when we dance it should be for Him.

Pastor, author and national Christian speaker, Louie Giglio, states in his book, *Wired for a Life of Worship*, that worship is our response to what we value the most. We worship *something* in everything that we do. Through our dance ministry, we are teaching young people how to worship God instead of other things (including themselves) when they dance. There is something very powerful about watching a room full of teenagers worshipping God through dance and not being shy about their faith.

Making It Work for You

Chapter 2

What Does Leadership Think?

Before you can start a dance program in your church, you absolutely must have leadership's approval and support. If, after reading this book and presenting the idea to them, they don't support the idea, then you cannot move forward. I say this because as long as you are part of a church you fall under the umbrella of their leadership. Maybe the timing isn't right or maybe they just need the right information to make a good decision for your church. Just trust God and pray for an opportunity to show itself.

If you're not sure where leadership stands, then make sure you are properly prepared before approaching them. The worst thing you could do is present the idea and be unprepared for questions and challenges.

Presenting Your Idea

When working on your presentation, make sure you take into consideration your church's mission and vision. Some people have a hard time understanding that in many ways their church is run like a business. Before a Senior Pastor or Board will sign off on adding a major ministry (especially one that will be visible in the congregation and community), they have to look at the benefits of such a program and make sure that it lines up with their corporate vision.

The following are some other things you should consider before presenting your ministry idea:

> What are your church's demographic & the demographics of the community?
>
> How active are your children and/or youth ministries?
>
> Will you use the dance program as an outreach? If so, how?
>
> How will a dance ministry further your church's mission?
>
> What financial and facility resources will be necessary?

Reasons to Add the Dance Program

Although each organization's reasons to add their dance ministry will differ slightly, I've put together some things that you may choose to incorporate into your plan.

- First and foremost, dance is an incredible form of worship and praise to the Creator of the Universe, who also created music and dance! In the first several pages of this book you were given several of the Biblical reasons that dance can be considered a legitimate form of worship.

- Like it or not, the church is competing against the "world" for our children's attention. That doesn't mean that we have to be "of" the world; however, we do have to live "in" it. We are fooling ourselves if we think that we can catch and keep an unchurched kid or teen's attention if we are not using tools that attract them until they are at a place where they are seeking God themselves.

- Music is a universal language. Don't believe it? Just go into a crowd of people and start playing music with a good beat. Almost immediately, people will begin tapping their feet and moving to the rhythm of the music.

- If you come from a church that has a strong 'outreach' effort, then they shouldn't even need to be convinced that this is a program to have active within your children and youth ministries. Outreach is all about going out into the community—where the unchurched live—and bringing them the Good News in a way that relates to them. Contemporary music meets people where they live and bridges the gap between them and the Church.

Reaching Today's Youth

In just about every youth or children's ministry magazine available, you can find studies and surveys quoting how many of our young people are having sex, drinking, cutting, purging, drugging, and living lives of reckless abandonment. Just open the newspapers and talk with the administrators of public schools and you'll find even more. During a blood drive in our local community, one of the high schools couldn't use over 80% of the donated blood because of sexually transmitted disease. This is not a large city—it's Middle America.

I've probably lost several of you at this point because I'm talking about things that are uncomfortable, like drugs and sex. But the reality is that this is what your kids are talking about. And not just your teenagers. Kids as young as 4th and 5th grade are beginning to be exposed to things that would surprise you. Even shock you.

This isn't limited to public schools, either. Parents whose children are enrolled in private schools in our area are also faced with the fact that their kids are exposed to sex, drugs and gangs and some are choosing to partake. These are kids from Christian homes who at one point in their lives lived for Jesus. What has happened? They've been exposed to the lies of Satan, and because those lies were wrapped in a package that looked good and seemed like fun, they decided at some point that it must be okay. We are fighting a battle and we have to use every tool in our arsenal to win!

Reaching today's kid or teen is not as easy as it used to be. Statistics show that most of them come from broken homes. Broken homes often produce broken people and reaching them requires you to be real with them. They need to hear how God is REAL and how He can move in their situation. But many of them will never hear that message because this generation is staying away from church in staggering numbers. We have to figure out what will grab their attention long enough to hear the Word so that they can see how God's grace and love is sufficient. We've chosen a dance program as one way to do this.

Several of the kids involved in our dance program have experienced real life-change as a result of being involved. Was it only our dance moves or the music we chose? No. It was the fact that we cared enough to bring them together for a common purpose and then invested in their lives. In the process of learning choreography and listening to positive music, they developed relationships with believers and were challenged to grow spiritually through our weekly devotions. We have used every opportunity to make this ministry a place where they could find Jesus and develop their gifts and talents along the way. We invite them to participate in our Youth and Children's services, which are relevant and interesting. We've included them in our small groups and youth events, encouraging them to get involved even if their parents don't come to our church. The bottom line is we do our best to show them the love of Jesus.

I have to issue a word of caution here and say that your church needs to be prepared for the results of using this type of program as an outreach tool. If you are using this style of music and dance as the "bait" when you are out in the community, then those kids you reach will be looking for some of that same flavor within the walls of the church's youth and kids programs. To put it in food terms, you can't attract them with a banana split and then only offer vanilla ice cream when they show up at your house.

How to Start

On Your Mark...
Get Set...
GO!

Chapter 3

How To Start

This chapter is designed to give you an idea of how you might choose to structure your dance program. The key word is "idea." The most important thing you could do to ensure the success of your program is to prayerfully look at your resources and work within your own boundaries. God will show you the best way to do this as long as you keep Him the focus. However, this chapter will give you some things to consider as you get started.

Ministry vs. Studio

If you have several years experience operating or teaching in a dance studio, beware. Starting a hip hop dance ministry and running a dance studio are two different things. If your goal is outreach, your dance program will have to be offered year-round with several opportunities throughout the year for the kids to perform. This is a little different than the September through May programs and end-of-the-year recitals that most studios offer.

You should also not expect a studio-like atmosphere in your classes. Although one can always hope, for some reason this type of program doesn't seem to provide for a quiet, orderly, class-like atmosphere. In fact, we have found that when we tried to demand that type of behavior every week, we began to lose kids. They want to have FUN dancing, and when it's too much like "work" we start to lose them. At least until they mature a little. All of that being said, we don't serve a God of chaos and there's nothing wrong with encouraging order. You'll just have to make sure that you're balancing order with fun. In our ministry the kids are much more responsive to a hard-line approach to discipline as we get closer to performance time.

Dance Experience

Having a great deal of formal dance training is not necessary to start a program like this. Nor is the ability to choreograph. All you really need is a passion for dance, ability in this style of dance and the right resources. If you don't feel as if you have adequate ability, take a look at the Resource section at the end of this book. I've provided some resources that can help you find choreography that will keep the kids' attention and at the same time be family-friendly. Now, let's see how to get started.

ON YOUR MARK— Pick Your Team

What age group you choose to start with will depend upon the ministry in which you are already involved or by direction of leadership. Some of you may already have a group of kids that want to get started and you're using this book to give you fresh ideas. However, if you are starting from scratch without any predetermined age requirements, I strongly suggest that you start with a group of kids that are within 2-3 years of each other. You can add additional age groups as appropriate. Let me explain why. If you start with ten kids that vary in age from 9 years old up to 19 years old, you have to take into consideration the fact that they have different dance abilities, as well as different music interests. Keeping everyone on the same page is going to be tough and will be a challenging way to start a new program.

Of course, some of you may already have a group of kids with whom you've been given to work, and you can still be successful. Just start with a song that allows you to use one age group for the verses and another age group for the chorus. Structuring your dance this way allows your choreography to be adapted to the abilities of the various age groups.

If you are starting from scratch and have total control over which age group to start with, a good group is 8—10 year olds. Some of you may want to start with teenagers, and if you have a good core group that will be easy to work with, go for it. We chose to start with a younger age group because they were the ones that were most willing to try something new. We didn't have to worry about teens and their reluctance to do something that may not fit in with their image or schedules. (We started our teen groups as the younger kids grew older — our program has successfully grown up with the kids.)

To get things going once you've decided on an age group, you'll want to recruit five to ten kids that you think will not be inhibited and with whom you want to work. Start by personally talking with their parents and explaining that you are starting a small dance group. Make sure the parents are committed to providing transportation and the funds necessary for dance outfits.

GET SET — Pick Your Time and Place

Choose a time and place each week that you will hold rehearsal. Don't be discouraged if you don't have a studio-type setting. We started with 4 kids in my family room on two Saturday mornings a month. Once we decided to start rehearsing for an Easter performance, we recruited six more kids and had rehearsals in the church's nursery during the Tuesday night adult choir rehearsal. Work with your own resources. Once you've set a date, have an orientation meeting with the kids and their parents, explaining the purpose of the new dance program and what they can expect for practices and potential performances.

GO!

No doubt you've heard the acronym, K.I.S.S. - Keep It Simple Silly. The worst thing you could do is complicate things at the beginning. If possible, start having practices long before there will be an expectation to perform. Then you'll have time to build your group of kids into a team.

If you start with a younger group, you'll need to spend some time working on the basics of hip hop dance, while at the same time building a strong spiritual foundation and a sense of "team." We started by working on isolations and getting the kids moving in a uniform manner. We had them walk across the floor with a hip hop flair, making them really stretch outside of their comfort zone. Then we'd work on getting everyone working on the same "levels" so that if we had a move that required them to bend their knees to "level 2" then everyone did the same thing. Next we taught isolated movements and finally moved toward combinations.

Those types of exercises are key to making sure that the team begins working together. Stick with the basics — it's something that we have to remind ourselves to do now that we've grown into a larger ministry so that we never lose track of the things we did at the beginning to become successful.

In the beginning, classes should last 60 to 90 minutes, with 20 to 30 minutes being devoted to spiritual growth. You must use this window of opportunity to unify the group of kids into a team, all understanding the importance of glorifying God in all they do, including dance. Here's an idea of how a typical 60 minute class may look:

2 minutes	Welcome & opening prayer
10 minutes	Warm-up and stretching
25 minutes	Isolations & new choreography
20 minutes	Devotion
3 minutes	Closing prayer

If you schedule 90 minute classes, then you can add an additional 10 minutes to the devotion and an additional 20 minutes to your isolations and new choreography.

When it comes time to make final preparations for a performance, you should be prepared for a couple things. First, you'll probably need extra rehearsals to build excellence into your performance. During these rehearsals a full devotion is not necessary; however, we always spend a few minutes reminding the team why they are dancing and praying for God to reveal Himself and help us dance with excellence.

Also, as their leader and teacher, be prepared to dance with the kids. Especially when they first start performing. Try to position yourself so they can see you, but so that you're not detracting from them. At our church, we have a raised stage so the teacher of our younger teams can stand on the floor in front of the kids and lead them without blocking the parents' view of their children. When the teens dance, we often have our adult leaders dance with them. This is for two reasons. The first is quality. Because we learn the dances well, it is often necessary to place us strategically throughout the group so that the overall performance is balanced and/or improved, depending on the group that is dancing. Secondly, the kids like it. When we dance with them it helps unify the team and takes away any excuses from kids who are concerned about how they look. When they start downplaying their ability, I can simply look at them and say, "If I can do this, so can you!"

Another thing to think about is what the team will wear. It's not necessary to go crazy with expensive costuming like you might see at a dance recital. Remember, we're trying to reach people in the community and show how much fun we can have dancing for the Lord. Going overboard with costuming can be very intimidating for some and prevent them from wanting to get involved. When we dance at our church and youth functions, we usually coordinate colors or ask the kids to purchase an inexpensive solid-color t-shirt and wear jeans. Although for Easter and Christmas, we wear black pants to dress it up a little. For outreach events in the community, we usually wear our Firehouse t-shirts and jeans, to advertise our youth center. Personalize your look for your team, but remember to Keep It Simple Silly!

Ten Keys to a Successful Program

Chapter 4

The following are ten keys that we have found will help keep your dance program moving in a positive direction. Establishing and maintaining momentum will require a little concentration in each of these areas:

Key 1: Keep God the Focus

Resolve right now to never stop pointing the kids toward God. In all that you do in your ministry, He must be the focus. You're probably saying, "Well... duh! I knew that." However, knowing it and doing it are two different things. Let me explain.

We humans have a bad tendency to pursue God with all of our might when _we_ need Him. When we want to chase our dreams, open a new business, have children, fix a marriage problem, or receive a financial miracle we don't have a problem at all having regular communication with our Creator. It's when things are going well and there are no major crises that we gradually look to our own resources instead of His.

I don't have a problem being honest with you and saying that I've dealt with this in my life and in this dance program. As someone who pursues excellence in all that I do, I have lost balance and proper perspective in my daily walk with God. How? By forgetting that it was God and not me that got us here. By making decisions on my own and beginning to lead us in a direction that _I_ thought we should be going, rather than seeking God's will first. By getting impatient with God and making things happen out of His timing, which never works as well as it would if I had just waited on Him.

The Bible is very clear about this one - Seek God FIRST, above all other things, and He will provide for your every need. (Matthew 6:33) Not only should you keep Him the focus of your plans for this program, but you should also keep Him the focus of every rehearsal and performance. Two of the things that we started doing from the very beginning are open and close in prayer and share a time of Devotion. Many times we've asked one of the kids to participate in this process by leading prayer or the Devotion. It doesn't just model the concept of putting God first, but teaches them how to apply it as well.

 Key 2: Enthusiasm

Nobody wants to be involved in something that's boring and dull—especially kids and teens! You have to generate a sense of anticipation for every week's practice so they know that they'll miss something if they don't show up.

The key to this "key" is YOU! As the leader of an organization, YOU are the temperature gauge, the one who determines how excited the kids will be about coming out to practice. Get prayed up before you arrive, asking the Holy Spirit to help you set the right attitude for the rehearsal, always keeping Him the focus.

When you start rehearsal, make sure that you get the kids psyched up about dancing for Jesus and keep the energy levels high during the rehearsal. Yell out, "How is everybody doing today?!?" and don't accept anything less than a loud, positive response. If they are weak in their response, ask it again. Then ask them if they're ready to 'Dance for Jesus' or 'Stomp Satan in the Dirt' or something age appropriate that gets them fired up. Choose a fast-paced praise song for the first part of your warm-up. It will get the adrenaline going.

Surprise them every once in a while with a bit of candy or some sort of treat, and always keep the dream out in front of them. Talk about when they will perform and how great it's going to be to show their families all that they've learned.

Be a living example of Romans 12:11- *"Never be lacking in zeal, but keep your spiritual fervor, serving the Lord."* The kids will follow your lead on this one.

Key 3: TEAMwork

If your church is like ours, most of the kids don't live in the same neighborhood. Because of that, they go to different schools, play on different sports teams, and the only time they see each other is at church. It will be imperative that you develop a TEAM mentality. You've heard the acronym before - **T**ogether **E**veryone **A**chieves **M**ore. All of you working together is the ONLY way that the dance team will look unified during a performance. The willingness to work together will come more naturally as they get to know each other and become friends.

If your team needs some additional help in this area, here are some things to consider doing during practices:

- Team building games. Split your group into two teams of 4-5 kids and play games like the "Telephone game" or a scavenger hunt where the team that works together the best wins. The phone game is also a great way to teach a lesson on gossip and rumors. You can find more team building ideas in the Resource section of this book.

- Pray for them. Ask for prayer requests and praise reports from the kids. Genuinely pray for them out loud at each rehearsal so that they know they are an important part of your team.

- Keep in touch. If someone misses a rehearsal, send them a card letting them know that they are missed. Once a month, celebrate all of the birthdays from that month with some cookies or cupcakes. How much money you spend isn't important—it's that you took the time to let them know you cared.

- Create a friendly environment. Even in a group of 6 or 8 kids, someone can feel left out. Make sure that each week you move kids around in your rehearsal line up so that they are not standing next to the same person each time. Encourage the kids to welcome new dancers and get to know each other.

Key 4: Create a Sense of Ownership

Kids will put a lot more effort into taking care of things that they bought with their own money than something that was just given to them. It's like that with the dance program as well. If you are purposeful about creating a sense of ownership within them, they will work that much harder at consistently coming to rehearsals, learning the dance moves, participating in fund raisers, etc. Getting the kids to feel this way about the dance program is not hard. Just get them involved! Give some of the older and more outgoing members the job of praying or giving the Devotion. Have others keep attendance or a record of the finances. When the kids have an active part in the group, they will begin treating it like it's their own and take it much more seriously.

Another way to do this is to get them involved in choreography. Occasionally during your rehearsals, get everyone into a large circle and start with 4 counts of choreography. Then the next person has to repeat those 4 counts and add 4 more, and so on around the circle. By the end you will have several 8 counts of choreography that you can use in one of your dances. It promotes unity and at the same time teaches them how to get involved in the choreography process.

Key 5: Raise Up Leaders Within

One of the natural results of creating a sense of ownership with your team is that within a short period of time, a few of your kids will rise up and begin showing signs of leadership. When we first started our program, we had one adult leader working with our kids.

After a few performances, the group began to grow and we realized that we probably needed to split into two age groups. Our director at the time recognized the fact that she could run both classes without a problem, but it would be much wiser to set up the future of our program by beginning the process of training a couple of our older kids to teach the younger class. She started by just having them lead the devotions and the warm up. Then she asked them to work with her on choreography. Within 2-3 months, the two girls were completely leading their class and all they needed was an adult leader to assist.

Currently, we have three adults in addition to me who are actively involved in our dance classes. However, we are really working with our teen leaders, encouraging them to take leadership seriously and begin to grow into young men and women who have been called by God. Those teens now choreograph most of our dances and teach the weekly classes with adult supervision.

There are many different ways to raise up leaders within an organization, and many books have been written that explain it in great detail. Our Pastor has stated for years that you are the sum of the information you allow to enter your mind through various books and tapes. He has set an incredible example of raising up leaders through monthly meetings he holds for all of his Ministry Coordinators. Those of us involved in ministry in our church are required to attend these rallies, where we receive great leadership training, vision casting and specific calendar planning. Most of the meeting is focused on the first two items, which keeps us all on point with our corporate vision.

We used this same model in establishing our "core" group or Ministry Team, as we call it. This group of leaders within our program is responsible for making things happen. All but a couple of them are teenagers, who have had very little leadership training outside of what we give them. Therefore, we constantly look for resources to share with them that teach the basic principles of leadership in a way that will relate to their age group.

Here are a couple resources that have worked for us:

- Personality profiling books are great at helping kids understand basic temperaments and why people behave the way they behave. *Personality Plus* by Florence Littauer has been around a while, but she does a great job putting things into terms the kids will understand, plus there's a little test in the book that helps them determine their particular traits.

- *Five Love Languages* by Gary Smalley is another good book that will help you teach the kids to understand how to show love toward other teammates. Not romantic love, but the type of love for one another that Jesus commanded us to show in Matthew 22:39. Although this is a book written for married couples, it helps with all of your relationships. As you read this book and realize that one of your dancer's primary love language is "words of affirmation" then you'll understand how mindlessly criticizing him during a rehearsal without carefully measuring your words can make him feel like you don't care.

- *Heart of the Artist* by Rory Nolan is a great book for artistic, creative people who are using those talents in ministry. Although he is the Music Director for Willow Creek Community Church in Illinois, he addresses all of the arts, including dance and drama. Rory reminds us to keep things in perspective and not allow the "artistic temperaments" to get out of balance. The book is written is such a way that it is great for small group lessons, although it's geared for older readers and not small children.

- Take your leaders to outside conferences that either feed their spirit or their dance ability, or both. There are several

Christian conferences around the country for praise and worship styles of dance, but most only touch briefly on contemporary styles such as hip hop as a style of dance that can be used within the church. In the Resource section of this book I've listed the ones that we have attended that were very helpful. Do some research and try to find others in your area that may be helpful as well.

Key #6: Strive for Excellence

Excellence. I could write an entire book on this subject because I think too many churches have settled for too long, accepting "good enough." Especially in kid and youth programs. Let me remind you that we are literally in a spiritual war—fighting for the souls of our youth. Why not use the best weapons available to gain and keep their attention on the things of God? If they have a choice between going to a secular concert where the sound and lighting is tight, multi-media abounds and the energy levels are high or a Christian outreach at a local church where the hand-me-down sound equipment is cracking and ringing and the singing and dancing are mediocre, what do you think they'd choose? What would *you* choose?

I told you that I could write a whole book on this subject and maybe I will one day, but here's the breakdown of why this is listed as one of the Keys to a Successful Program.

First and foremost, *anything* that we do for God should be done with the highest levels of excellence that we can possibly produce... just because it's being done for Him. I don't know about you, but I want my Creator and Father to know that I love him enough to give Him my very best, not just "good enough."

The second reason that excellence should be pursued is because of what I said earlier. We are in a spiritual battle and we shouldn't strive for anything less than what the world has to offer. This is a tough one. Not just because excellence is hard to achieve, but because there is a delicate balance that needs to be maintained when establishing excellence in ministry. Especially if, like us, you are working with kids and teens who have had little to no prior dance experience. One of the things that we always have to remember is that regardless of how big we grow or how good we become, we are still a ministry within our church, whose mottos is "Love, Acceptance and Forgiveness." We always love and accept all kids into our program, whether they have rhythm or not, and whether they are living lives dedicated to God or not. It's our job to help them dance the best they can and modify our choreography to include every level of ability. It's also our job to help them discover how to live a life for God.

Also remember that excellence doesn't mean perfection. None of us are perfect. But God is blessed when our intentions are pure and as long as we are giving our very best to Him, He honors those efforts.

Key #7: Be Flexible!

If you've not read it yet, you should definitely read the book *Who Moved My Cheese?* by Spencer Johnson. It's a quick read, only about an hour, but it will help you to understand the importance of not getting so set in your ways that you are unable to move quickly when change happens. Notice that I said _when_ change happens. We all know that it will—it's just a matter of when.

How does that relate to your dance program? Because your program exists to support the efforts of the youth or kids programs and they exist to support the efforts of the church. You're bound to have changes thrown at you. For instance, a change in the class schedule because someone needs the rehearsal space on *your* night. Or being asked to "throw together" a quick something for service next week. Or being told the day before a performance that you won't be needed. The key is to remember that you are part of a larger organization that needs you to be flexible... without grumbling.

Robert Schuller has an incredible quote that touches on attitude, which I think fits well in this section:

> *"The longer I live, the more I realize the impact of attitude on life. Attitude, to me, is more important than facts. It is more important than the past, than education, than money, than circumstances, than failure, than successes, than what other people think or say or do. It is more important than appearance, giftedness or skill. It will make or break a company... a church... a home. The remarkable thing is that we have a choice everyday regarding the attitude we will embrace for that day. We cannot change our past... we cannot change the fact that people will act in a certain way. We cannot change the inevitable. The only thing we can do is play on the one string we have, and that is our attitude. I am convinced that life is 10% what happens to me and 90% how I react to it. And so it is with you... we are in charge of our Attitudes."*

One of the things our kids will hear me say when they start grumbling about changes that they don't like is that "It's not about you. It's about Him and it's about them." For us, the *them* is the other kids that we're trying to reach and the *Him* is Christ and whether or not we're giving Him glory by being so rigid in our ways.

Key #8: Never Compromise Your Values

There are two strong messages in the first two verses of Romans 12 that I continually speak to our dance teams. I've already discussed the first one, Romans 12:1— *"offering our bodies as living sacrifices, as this is our spiritual worship."*

In the next verse, however, Paul encourages us to *"not conform to the pattern of this world."* Because we are using this culture's music and dance style, we are always in danger of crossing the line into the abyss of compromise, especially when you use Hip Hop to reach out to the community. Even watching Christian rap videos, I often see dance moves and costuming that I personally consider a compromise of the values God set for us in His Word.

One of the things our dance team will tell you is that I am a stickler for dress code. At rehearsals we ask the kids to stay away from shorts unless they are below the knee and we also insist on sleeved shirts. Privately, I'll tell the girls, "No Butts, No Bellies and No Breasts. There are just some body parts that only your spouse should see." The intention of these kinds of rules is not to box people into how I think a Christian should dress. They are to prevent opportunities for Satan to sneak in and cause problems by distracting the kids away from learning about how to worship God through dance.

Another area that we are always mindful of is our dance moves. There is no place for sensuality in a dance ministry. For us, that means that any overt thrusting of the chest or hips is forbidden. Sometimes just a slight adjustment of a dance move makes it appropriate and still keeps it relevant to today's dance style.

One specific style of dance that I am cautious about in our dance program is Krumping. While many of the versions are not overtly sexual, almost every version has some hip or chest thrusting that just isn't acceptable in ministry.

God called us to be a light in a dark place (Matthew 5:14) and that means that sometimes we have to make a choice to behave differently. Living in the world and ministering to the people of the world doesn't equate to becoming part of the world. You just have to make the decision to not compromise - period.

 Key #9: Communicate Well

I can't stress enough how important this is to retaining a

consistent team. Turnover is usually caused because someone's feelings got hurt when they weren't told about a rehearsal or one that got cancelled. Or they couldn't perform because they didn't wear the right outfit that day.

Keeping kids, and more importantly, their parents, informed of all of your activities is absolutely necessary to keeping a strong forward momentum in your dance program. How do you do that? Follow the old adage - "Put it in writing!"

We have a *"Dates to Remember"* postcard that I print and give to all of the kids and their parents so they can post it on their refrigerator. In addition, I send regular emails to the dancers and their parents to remind them of upcoming rehearsals and performances.

We also have a MySpace page. I know that some of you will gasp in horror, but let's be "real" for a minute. Kids have MySpace pages and most of them check that site more than they check their email. You can choose to stick your head in the sand and pretend that "your" kids won't visit MySpace, but the reality is that they do. So you can either use that venue to your benefit or pretend it doesn't exist and miss great opportunities to not only communicate, but to also see what your kids are doing. Not to mention the fact that if your program is focused on reaching the unchurched community, then you absolutely have to use the tools that will relate to them.

Anyone involved in our core group or Ministry Team is required to add me as a "friend" so I can monitor what they are communicating on their personal website. On several occasions I've been able to suggest changes to their space and use what I see to open up good conversations with the kids. Just be careful to not put too much info on your page regarding locations and times of your rehearsals. Make interested parties contact you directly for that information rather than offering it to anyone who sees the page. Our MySpace page is www.MySpace.com/FireDancePSL. Go check it out and see how we choose to stay in touch.

Here are some of the other things that we do to keep in touch with our dancers and their parents:

- *We Miss You* postcards are sent to dancers when they've missed a class. They are easy to produce on your computer and cost only a few cents for a stamp and cardstock paper. Many times parents have told me that their child was really touched because they received a card from the dance team.
- *Newsletters* — parents and kids love to receive the newsletters, especially when we highlight a particular person or group and add pictures. It's a great thing for them to keep in their scrapbooks and keeps the successes and goals out in front of everyone all the time. Again, nothing fancy. Just a little something produced on your own computer will suffice. We use Microsoft Publisher because we have regular access to it, but any word processing program will work great. Remember, it's about communicating information not just producing a pretty newsletter.
- Of course, the low-tech *phone call* is always a great way to make sure everyone has the info, and it's personal. Since having things in writing keeps the miscommunication down to a minimum, we do both.

Tip #10: Have Fun!

This seems like a no-brainer, but the busier you get and the more you are exposed to the emotional rollercoaster of adolescence, you run the risk of getting bogged down in the "work" and forget to have fun.

If we start to feel like we're getting run down from all of the activity, we have a party. No agenda, just a time to dance around, eat and have fun. Or we'll go see a movie together. There have been several good dance movies produced over the years, so you could bring everyone together and watch it on a big screen television with popcorn. Nothing expensive, just something that lets everyone on your team take a deep breath and relax.

A large part of having fun is to remember *why* you are doing this. It all goes back to setting your sights on God and letting <u>Him</u> be the reason you dance. When you begin to lose that focus, you immediately get out of balance. Stay in tune with God's purpose for your dance program and He will point you in the right direction.

Opportunities for Ministry

Chapter 5

Now that you have started a dance team, what on Earth will you do with them? For some of you the answer has been provided by your church leadership. For others, you have much more flexibility with your team. Here are a few ways you can use your dance team to gain visibility in your church and in your community:

Outreach Events

This is the real beauty of having a contemporary dance program in your church. There are endless opportunities to reach out into the community and use the dance team to point people toward your church. In fact, after just a few outreaches, you'll start getting phone calls from other people to perform. Before you know it, you'll have to pick and choose which events are the best for you to attend.

Here's a list of some of the types of opportunities you should look for in your community:

- Parades (Christmas, 4th of July, Martin Luther King Day, etc.)
- Lighting of the Tree ceremonies at Christmas time
- Local festivals and fairs
- Opening day of various sports activities
- Half-time shows during playoff games at community sports activities
- Ethic festivals, such as Greek Festival, Italian Festival, etc. Most communities have several of these during the course of the year
- Fundraising events for national organizations such as the American Cancer Society's Relay for Life, the Avon Walk for Breast Cancer or local Crisis Pregnancy Center events.

Get your group's name out there in the community and before long you'll start seeing new visitors in your dance classes and in your church.

Youth Events

Everyone does this differently, but if your youth group is actively seeking ways to reach the unchurched youth in your community, then you are probably already hosting various youth activities. Concerts, skateboard competitions, dance-offs, singing competitions, paintball competitions, etc., are all great examples of this. Anytime you host something for the youth, have the dance team show up for at least one dance to kick things off. It increases the energy level of the event and the exposure of your team.

Make sure that regardless of which of these forums you use for getting your dance team exposure, you keep seeking counsel from your church's leadership. Your job is to <u>support</u> their goals, so communication with them is important.

Church Events

The dance team is an obvious fit for things like Easter and Christmas. Especially if you have kids and/or youth programs at those times of the year. At our church, we have special kids programs the week before Easter and the week before Christmas, which is a great time to highlight the dance teams. It adds a lot of energy to the service and often brings in the parents of kids who participate in dance, but don't regularly attend our church.

The dance team can also be used for other church events, such as the church's anniversary, Independence Day, Grandparent's Day, Dinner on the Grounds, etc.

If you have kid and youth services that are separate from the adults, you have many opportunities to work the dance team into the praise and worship time. We try to work something into our youth services at least once a month. It allows us to build excitement during the services and it also provides more opportunities for the kids to dance in front of other people. The more they perform, the less nervous they feel each time they get on stage.

Don't forget what I said earlier about reaching today's youth. If you use the music from today's culture in outreach efforts but only play Chrisitan music that was popular 20 years ago, you're going to lose a lot of the kids you reach. That would be a shame, especially when there are so many good ways to use current technology in your kid and youth programs. For instance, you could have Christian music videos playing before service starts, or have a message illustrated by using a music video. The internet has a great deal to offer as well, and I don't just mean the conventional "youth program" websites that provide so many great resources. If you go to www.YouTube.com and search using the words "Christian" or "Bible" you'll come up with some great amateur videos to which the kids can really relate. You could even have the dance team make up their own and play it during service. Don't be afraid of today's culture... embrace it and use it to God's advantage.

A Final Word of Encouragement

So, no matter how you do it, get out there and dance for God's glory! You'll be amazed at the doors He will open for you once you've taken the initial step of faith. My prayer is that this book has been helpful to you in your quest to start or expand your dance program. From experience, I know that it can be overwhelming at times, but as long as you keep God the center, your program will be healthy and productive.

As you establish and grow your program, I'd love for you to stay in touch and keep me updated on your progress. Email me at: Info@IgniteAFirestorm.com.

Here are some pictures of our Ministry Team and a few of the opportunities that we've been given to minister over the years. I can't wait to see your pictures!

FireDance Ministry Team – 4/07

Dancing for Jesus is a blast!!

Dancing at a Firehouse Youth Centre function

Taking a break from rehearsals

Working on a breakdancing pose

2006 Firehoue Youth Centre dance competition

Ministering at Real Life Kids Ranch in Okeechobee, FL

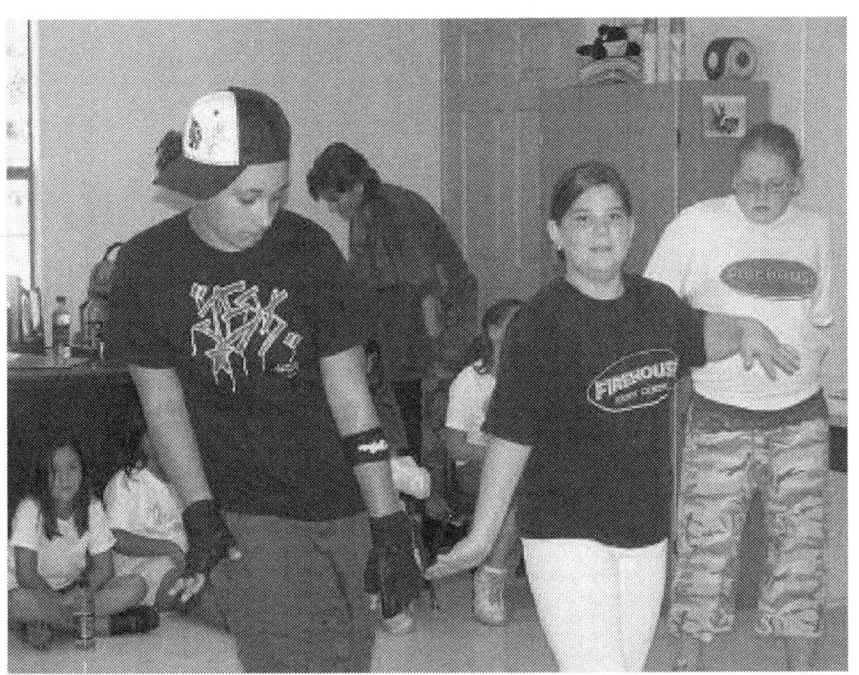
Teaching a "battle" class at Dance Camp

Getting ready for the final showcase of Dance Camp

Resources

Team Building Games

Here are some of the team-building games and ice breakers that you can use for your dance program. There are so many resources available to help you find more of these types of games, but here are a few to get you started.

<u>Telephone Game</u>: Separate your team into two or three smaller groups, with at least 6-7 kids in each group. Have each group stand single file, but not within earshot of the other groups. Give the first person in each line a small piece of paper that says the same thing. Make sure the paragraph has at least 5-6 lines and provides some details. An example would be, "Ms. Kelli bought a new house with a pool. She and her family of 5 went swimming in the blue pool with purple floaties and yellow fins. After they finished, they danced the Hokey Pokey with 6 of their friends until it got dark." Make it a fun.

The people to whom you gave the paper have 15 seconds to read the paragraph and then they have to give it back to you. It is then their job to tell the person next to them exactly what that paper said, whispering so that no one else hears. Then the second person tells the third person, and so on. By the time the message is passed to the last person in each line, it has probably been distorted to something other than what was written.

Have the last person in each group tell everyone what they heard. After all of the groups have reported, read the paragraph that the first person of each group received. Use this as an opportunity to teach about gossip and how messages can quickly become distorted from their original intent. Give a reward to the group that kept the purest message.

Getting To Know You: With all of the dancers in a large circle, have one person start by giving their name and one interesting thing about themselves that not everyone knows. Then the next person in the circle will repeat the first person's name and information and add their own name and interesting information. That continues around the circle until it gets back to the first person, who has to name everyone in the circle and the one thing about them no one knew.

Find Your Group: Hand everyone a piece of paper that has the following things typed out. Have them get as many people's signatures as possible in each category, giving them only as much time as it takes to listen to a 3-4 minute song. Whoever has the most verified signatures, wins.

- Find 3 people who have blond hair.
- Find 3 people who have white shoes.
- Find out 5 people's middle names.
- Find out 3 people who live in your same ZIP code.
- Find 2 people who have blue shoes.
- Find 2 people who were born in the city in which you live.
- Find 3 people who were born in the state in which you live.
- Find 2 people who were born out of state.
- Find 3 people who have more than 3 siblings.

<u>Alphabet Game</u>: Write the letters of the alphabet down the side of the paper (you can exclude X, Q and Z if you want). Next to each letter, draw a long line. Give the kids 5-6 minutes to find out something about other dancers that would fit with the letters. They can only use one person for 4 of the letters. This is what the first part of the page may look like:

A <u>**T**ommy likes to eat **A**pples.</u>

B <u>**S**haron has a **B**and-Aid on her finger.</u>

C <u>**L**isa has a brother named **C**arlos.</u>

<u>Life Saver Game</u>: Pair the kids up, trying to keep girls with girls and boys with boys, if possible. Also, encourage the kids to *not* pair with their best friend. Give each person a long drinking straw or a long stick (like a arts & crafts dowel) that is approximately the same size as a straw. Then, have them put the straw in their mouth and place a life saver on one of the partners' straws. The goal is to move the life saver from one person to another without using your hands. If the candy falls to the ground, that team is disqualified. Whoever does it the quickest wins. Another fun way to do this is to blind-fold one of the partners.

Devotion Ideas

The goal with the weekly devotions is to spend 10-15 minutes teaching a Godly principle and showing the kids how to pray for each other, by asking for prayer requests and praise reports. If you need ideas for devotions, there are many resources available for various age groups. Some of the topics we have used repeatedly over the past few years are highlighted below:

- Choices: We all have choices to make in our lives, and most people don't realize the spiritual impact of certain choices. We start this devotion by asking the kids to tell us which radio stations they listen to, and then to give us their favorite TV shows. Usually we get feedback about very secular music and TV shows with a great deal of bad attitude, language and sexual content. At this point we discuss Romans 12:2, where Paul encourages us to not conform to the world, but transform ourselves through the renewing of our minds. We explain the negative effect that results from continually listening to negative messages through TV and radio, adding several personal examples where applicable.

- Attitude: This is one of the principles that we address on a regular basis. Several really good books have been written that fully explore the importance of having a good attitude in all that we do. Make sure that you discuss things that relate back to the kids' lives and how they respond to difficult situations. Good topics are parents, school and responsibility.

- Sharing God's Love: In Matthew 28 Jesus commands us to love one another. It's a simple commandment, but not always so easy to show. We discuss ways that we can share God's love with our friends, parents, teachers, friends, relatives and neighbors. Give them all two pieces of paper that say "I thank God for you." Tell them to put one paper on their bathroom mirror so they see that message every morning and every night. Then ask them to give the other paper to someone for whom they are thankful.

- <u>Purity</u>: This is a subject that we start discussing in moderation with our 6th graders. We talk about appropriate dress and how what we wear can drastically affect the way others think about and treat us. *Secret Keeper 2005: The Delicate Power of Modesty* by Dannah Gresh is a great book to use for devotions on this subject. It's geared towards girls, but there's no reason boys can't be involved in the discussion. After all, if they are more careful about how they respond to girls and the way they dress and behave, then it would have a corresponding affect on how the girls choose to dress.

You can find several resources for devotional ideas that specifically speak to the age group of your team. Do some research in your local Christian bookstore and see what's out there. Just remember that the key is to promote life change within the kids, pointing them toward God.

Music Choices

This is truly the key to having a successful dance program and at the same time, making sure that the program is God focused. There has been much controversy over Christian artists using contemporary music to spread the message of Jesus Christ. You have to seek God on this one yourself and be comfortable with the music to which you are exposing your kids. There are so many different styles of contemporary music that you can use in your dance program. Here is a partial list of artists that we have used in our program:

Out of Eden	Jump 5
Mary Mary	True Vibe
LaCrae	Kirk Franklin
Martha Munizzi	Israel Houghton
Vicki Winans	Toby Mac
CeCe Winans	Clint Brown
Souljahz	Carmen
21:03	T-Bone
Tammy Trent	Ambassador
Zoe Girl	Audio Adrenaline
KJ-52	The Newsboys
Plus One	Stacie Orrico
J Moss	Cross Movement
Greg Hammond	da Truth

Do your research and make sure that the artist is leading a fruitful Christian life. I almost didn't include this list of artists because I didn't want to "date" this book, but also because people can fall into sin and in between the time these words are typed and you read this book, things could change in one of their lives. However, when people from other churches have called me for advice on how to proceed with their dance program, the issue of music is always included in their list of questions.

Obviously, you have to choose age appropriate songs that are also appropriate for the venue. Hopefully this will give you somewhere to start in your search, and I trust that the Holy Spirit will guide you to find the right music for your program.

Networking with other Christian dance groups is another key to finding good music and keeping up with the industry. Some of the organizations that I've listed in the next several pages of this section will be good resources for you. In addition, we have added a "Dancer's Forum" on our website (www.one-sourceproductions.com) for you to ask questions and discuss various issues relevant to your dance program. One of the subjects listed is Christian artists and music.

Dance Conferences

There are many praise and worship dance programs around the country, but we have found that very few focus more on contemporary styles of dance, such as hip hop and breakdancing. Below you will find what I'm sure is just a partial list of conferences, but ones of which we are familiar and can recommend:

Dance Revolution is a phenomenal conference geared toward dance studios, but a few ministry groups have begun attending as well. They teach classes on all styles of dance, but they have stepped up to the plate in offering hip hop, pop 'n lock and jazz funk classes that have really stretched our Ministry Team. The most incredible thing about Alec and Michelle Brogan and their staff is that there is NEVER a question about why and for whom they dance. God is the focus of the entire weekend. Find a regional conference close to you by visiting:

www.dance-revolution.com

Project Dance is a conference that started in New York City, but is now available in other cities as well. Like Dance Revolution, they gear their program toward studio dance teams, but they provide a great opportunity for outreach during their Showcase, which is usually performed at an outside venue. At the New York event, the Showcase is in the middle of Times Square – how cool is that!? Visit their website for additional information:

www.projectdance.com

Word in Motion Urban Dance Festival, based in California, is an all hip-hop Christian conference and showcase. Their classes range from hip hop to jazz funk to old school and they also have a Christian rap concert during the event. You can obtain more information regarding this conference at their website:

www.wordinmotion.com

Dance Ministry Magazine puts on an annual conference based in Ft. Pierce, FL, that is geared toward various styles of dance used in church services. They also incorporate sessions on hip hop dance and Christian rap. Visit their website at:

http://myweb.ecomplanet.com/mcac9535

Ignite! is a series of dance workshops that our FireDance Ministry Team provides to other church groups to help start a new dance program or give your existing program a fresh burst of energy. We customize a workshop specific to your needs; whether 1 or 2-day workshops for the kids, a 2 or 3-day Dance Intensive for your core group and stronger dancers or a weekend workshop for your leaders, helping you to get started. We are also available to perform for your church or youth group, so they can see the type of ministry that is possible for your organization. If you're interested, contact us for additional information.

www.firedancepsl.com

Instructional Videos

There are a lot of instructional dance videos available that can serve as inspiration for your choreography. Some are specifically choreographed for Christian songs, so you can use them as demonstrated. Others show simple hip hop moves that you can use as a starting point for your own choreography. Below is a partial list:

- **Jam X Kids**

    Available through bookstores and online at Amazon

- **Authority of Hip Hop**

    Available through: *www.dance-revolution.com*

- **Worship Steps**

    Available through their website:

    www.worshipsteps.com

- **P149**

    Available through their website: *www.P149.com*

- **Relentless**

    Available through: *www.relentlessinmotion.com*

- **Ignite NOW! Video Series**

    Available through: *www.one-sourceproductions.com*

    > The **Ignite NOW! Video I** *is designed specifically for beginning teams. We provide a great warm-up, an isolation routine and two performance dances in addition to a devotion designed to help new dancers understand how and why they should dance for God. You can get more information on this at our website.*

Thank you for purchasing this book. Look for additional resources coming soon from Kelli Moore and the FireDance team!

- **Fanning the Flames**: *A Year of Devotions and Other Tools for Your Dance Program.*

    This workbook will provide you with:
    - 52 weekly devotions
    - team-building games
    - ideas for fundraisers and dance parties
    - sample note cards and administrative forms
    - sample newsletters

- **Firestorms That Last**: *Structuring Your Dance Program for Growth and Longevity.*

    Once you've started a dance program, what's next? This follow-up to *Ignite a Firestorm* will provide guidelines for you to structure your program for growth and maximum effectiveness.

www.ingramcontent.com/pod-product-compliance
Lightning Source LLC
Chambersburg PA
CBHW021026090426
42738CB00007B/915